The Man Without A Country

The Man Without A Country

AND ITS HISTORY

EDWARD EVERETT HALE

Chapman Billies, Inc., Sandwich, MA

ISBN: 0–939218–08–8

Printed in the United States of America

Breathes there the man, with soul so dead,
Who never to himself hath said,
　　This is my own, my native land!
Whose heart hath ne'er within him burned,
As home his footsteps he hath turned,
　　From wandering on a foreign strand!
If such there breathe, go mark him well:
For him no Minstrel raptures swell;
High though his titles, proud his name,
Boundless his wealth as wish can claim;
Despite those titles, power, and pelf,
The wretch, concentred all in self,
Living, shall forfeit fair renown,
And doubly dying, shall go down
To the vile dust, from whence he sprung,
Unwept, unhonoured and unsung.

　　　　　　　　— WALTER SCOTT
　　　　　　　　The Lay of the Last Minstrel
　　　　　　　　Canto 6, stanza I

THE PUBLISHER of this edition of *The Man Without A Country* asks me to give some account of the circumstances and incidents of its publication. I do this with a certain reluctance, lest it should seem that I think they are more important than they are. It is true, however, that a series of curious coincidences accompanied the history of the story. Persons who are interested in the Curiosities of Literature, then, may read this preface — and other persons are under no compulsion to do so. The Civil War has taught its lesson so well that the average American of the year 1896 hardly understands that any such lesson was ever needed. The United States *is* a nation, now. And there is not left anyone, living in the Northern, Middle, Western, or Pacific states, who ever thinks that the United States *are* a confederacy. The war settled that. But in 1862 men were obliged to make speeches — to write pamphlets and books — to show what now seems of course. And any lesson was well received by persons of conscience and patriotism, which showed either positively or negatively what the word "patriotism" means — or what one's country is.

Among other persons who did not seem to know was an Ohio politician named Vallandigham.* Perhaps he is living still. The general reader of today would not know his name, but that in some address he said that he did not want to live in a country which did something or other which the National Administration, under Lincoln, had done. General Ambrose Everett Burnside was then in command of the Military Department in which Mr. Vallandigham lived. With a certain delicate wit and readiness which were characteristic of the man, Burnside marked his sense of the treasonable speech by sending Mr. Vallandigham with his compliments to the Rebel general on the other side of the Ohio, saying that we wanted no such people and that the Rebel States were welcome to him. The letter and the present which went with it of course engaged public attention in the region where the transfer was made. The Copperhead faction in Ohio, boldly and with good political shrewdness, as it seems to me, accepted the issue, and named Mr. Vallandigham — who was a martyr on their theory — as their candidate for governor in the next election. He was exactly the fit candidate on the issue then before the people.

I was, at this time, furnishing political articles for the

---

* Vallandigham, Clement Laird (1820–1871). Ohio Democrat congressman 1858–1863; supported states rights and reconciliation with the South; convicted of sedition for vehemence of opposition to the war; sentence commuted by Lincoln to banishment to the Confederacy, whence he went to Canada, returning to the North in 1864 to help write national Democratic Party platforms in 1864 and 1868.

Atlantic Monthly. I had already conceived the idea of the "Man Without a Country." I pressed the necessary work on it so that it might be published in the October number of the *Atlantic*, as my contribution to the Ohio canvass, as the election was to take place in October. But with a certain languor which attends the publication of most monthly journals — a languor which seems to me an infelicity — the publication was delayed until December, 1863, when Mr. Vallandigham had been beaten six weeks before by a majority of more than one hundred thousand — and forgotten, till now, as long.

I say the idea had been conceived many months before, not to say many years before.

Napoleon the Great always had an idea that he had surrendered himself at Rochefort to Captain Maitland of the ship *Bellerophon*, which ship received him after his overthrow. He sometimes undertook to maintain the absurd proposition that he was Maitland's personal captive, as in the Middle Ages one knight might have yielded himself as personal captive to another. This theory appears more than once in his invectives against the cruelty of the English government in holding him at St. Helena.

The proposition seems to me absurd. It seemed so to the English government, to the Prince Regent whom Napoleon addressed as "the most powerful, the most constant, and the most generous of my enemies." This was, by the way, the best thing the first gentleman in England ever had said of him — if only by good fortune it had been true. But whether absurd or not, it seems to me that it would have been good policy for the English Cabinet to have taken the fallen Emperor at his word. "Oh! you thought you were a guest on the *Bellerophon*? We did not understand it so, but a guest on the *Bellerophon* you shall be.

"Joiners, upholsterers, plumbers, painters — all of you — fly round — quick there — make ready a fine cabin — with sleeping rooms adjacent — for our distinguished guest, General Buonaparte. From this time he is the guest of the British people. He has come 'like Themistocles to seat himself by its hearth.' He has elected the *Bellerophon* as the place. So let it be." Then from cruise to cruise, of the *Bellerophon*," our distinguished guest would have been heard from thus:

NAVAL INTELLIGENCE

Sept. 30. H.M. Ship *Bellerophon* touched at the Cape, for water and mails. Our distinguished guest was in good health.

And then, six months after

June 11. Macao. H.M. Ship *Bellerophon* arrived for repairs, having lost a topmast in the typhoon. Our distinguished guest Gen. Buonaparte seemed to be well.

And, six months later

Dec. 11, Botany Bay. The corvette, Capt. Bell, reports that she spoke at sea H.M.S. *Bellerophon*. The *Bellerophon* made signal that all were well.

And so on, and so on. The "British people" could have stood it as long as the Emperor could.

What the British government did was to consecrate St. Helena as a shrine for the worship of France for the next six years. It won for itself a general odium, such as it does not dislike, among all the nations of Europe. But if the Cabinet had happened to hear my plan, and had executed it, many apologies for its cruelty would have been unnecessary. They could say, "We did just what the Emperor expected, and what he asked for."

I may say in passing, that the English cabinet has had more than one opportunity to take my advice, freely offered, and has, I think, always declined it.

Thus I had in my mind from the time when I read Scott's *Napoleon*, a book not forgotten in my youth, the plan on which the story of poor dear Phil Nolan is constructed—the story which is, at this present moment, in this reader's hands. The patriotic boys were singing a popular song, which said,

> "We'll hang Jeff Davis to a sour apple tree."

Jeff Davis, as it may not be remembered, was the leader of the Southern party. But I would say gently, "No, dear boys, we will not hang him to any tree. We will put him in comfortable quarters on the *New Hampshire* ship of the line, and we will send him on her serial three-year voyages. Where she goes he shall go, and where she stays he shall stay." Now the *New Hampshire* is a fine old square-sided, three or four decker, which is now a home for schoolboys, as may be seen by tourists in New York harbor. In those days she was thirty-three years newer or younger than she is now.

With such motives, with such resources, and such principles, I began to read for the story of "The Man Without a Country." I spent that summer in my old home at Worcester, a "Western town in the heart of New England." I used, almost every morning, to report to my old friend, Mr. Samuel Foster Haven, the Librarian of the Antiquarian Society, one of the wisest, one of the best-informed, and one of the best men who ever lived. Ah me! his fine son, a surgeon in the 15th Massachusetts, had been killed the year before, while marching with the regiment in the battle of Fredericksburg. I would pass the time of day with Mr. Haven, and then go into Salisbury Hall, and read up for "The Man Without a Country." As yet he had no name.

I read first the reports of the Navy Department from 1798, when it was still a branch of the War Department, down to 1861. This was to be sure of my local color, and that I might never, by any accident, place a vessel in the place where she really was, or name an officer so that a real man could be annoyed. Shaw's name, Shubrick's name in the story, are naval names — this was requisite for the color of the narrative. But there were no officers whom they fit. The *Levant* was a ship in our service. But she had disappeared — no man knows where — oh! years before I introduced her on the top of the Andes. I will here say — so careful are critics — that among many readers of this story, only one, of whom I ever heard, observed that the *Levant,* when Nolan died on her, was far inland. She had been placed on the top of the Andes intentionally .

I took such pains as this to be provided for defense, if any-one should say, as the *New York Observer* did courteously, that I was a liar and a counterfeiter. Liars and counterfeiters do not intentionally place ships on the tops of mountains, and none but very ignorant editors think they do.

I took full notes of the names of officers and ships, to be ready for the detail of my story. I then read, in full, all that I could find of Aaron Burr's two voyages down the Mississippi. It is not creditable to this country that there is no adequate history of Burr's attempt, whatever it was. I have sometimes thought that Mr. Jefferson himself did not wish to have any detail known. I am quite sure, after a good deal of study of the subject, that the officers of his Administration did not know every detail, nor one-half the details, nor one-fiftieth part of them.

The mines from which some competent historian will one day draw his most curious information as to Burr and his accomplices, are in the archives of the City of Mexico and of the cities of the Northern provinces of what was then the Viceroyalty of Mexico. Other information must be searched for in the city of Madrid. By a somewhat amusing accident, nearly forty years ago, the Spanish government, in sending to the State of Louisiana some documents relating to its early history, unintentionally revealed the fact that General James Wilkinson, who commanded our forces for many years in the valley of the Mississippi, and who made Burr think that he was his accomplice, was in fact for many years in the pay of the Spanish governor at

New Orleans. That government understood the knack of governing better than Mr. Jefferson and his friends, who thought at that time that the world was governed too much. While Burr was organizing his expedition, the Spanish government had its agents in every seaport city of the North. Their reports were faithfully transmitted to the governors of the Northern provinces, and some of them will be found in Santa Fé, in Austin, in San Antonio, in Monterey, and probably in Chihuahua, at this day.

Of all this, however, I knew nothing in the summer of 1863, nor did I need to know anything. I did read through the three volumes of General Wilkinson's *Memoirs*, a very stupid galimatias of facts and of lies. I also read through the proceedings of Burr's trial at Richmond; there are not many people in the world who can say that. In the Antiquarian Library it was easy to find the sidelights, particularly in the newspaper files. Thus the Antiquarian Library is the only place where I could examine the newspapers of the period, describing Burr's journeys. These files were useful for bits of local color — the name of a country-dance for instance.

The plan of the story is simple, and when once ready to write, I wrote it, with my own hand, as I wrote then, almost without break. At the place where the author changes, and the story comes from Danforth's pen instead of Ingham's, I sent the copy to Mr. Fields of the *Atlantic* to ask him if it would do, and to explain why it must be printed immediately, if at all, and why printed without my name, in absolute secrecy. Fields sent back word at once that it would do, and that if he could have the rest of the copy at once it could go into the next number. I did finish it at once, I think in one sitting. The sentimental reader may be interested to know that my own tears blotted the paper of the original manuscript.

Why it did not go into the October number nor the November number, I think I never knew. It was printed in the December number, about the middle of November. The first I knew of this was that I met James Freeman Clarke at an evening party, and he said to me, "Edward, we have been reading your story and we like it very much."

I said, "What story?"

He said, "The story of the Man Without a Country."

I said, "How did you know I wrote it ?"

Clarke said, "Because it says so in the index at the end of the number."

Between me and Fields the utmost caution had been observed that the article should be ascribed to Lieutenant Ingham, who is named as its author in the text. But the manuscript was in my handwriting, and the index-maker at Cambridge had not been consulted as to secrecy. He knew no reason why the world should not know what he knew, so in making the annual index, which goes with the December number, he innocently announced my name. Mr. Fields's wish, and mine, therefore, that the article might in some quarters be ascribed to a naval officer was balked from the beginning by a well-meant blunder in the printing office.

The story took the public eye and interest. It met the taste of the patriotic public at the moment. It was copied everywhere without the slightest deference to copyright. It was, by the way, printed much more extensively in England than it was in America. Immediately there began to appear a series of speculations based on what you would have said was an unimportant error of mine. My hero is a purely imaginary character. The critics are right in saying that not only there never was such a man, but there never could have been such a man. But he had to have a name. And the choice of a name in a novel is a matter of essential importance, as it proved to be here.

I had a hero who was a young man in 1807. He knew nothing at that time but the valley of the Mississippi River. "He had been educated on a plantation where the finest company was a Spanish officer, or a French merchant from Orleans." He must have a name familiar to Western people at that time. Well, I remembered that in these preposterous memoirs of Wilkinson's, whenever he had a worse scrape than usual to explain, he would say that the papers were lost when Mr. Nolan was imprisoned or was killed in Texas. This Mr. Nolan, as Wilkinson generally calls him, had been engaged with Wilkinson in some speculations mostly relating to horses and almost always disreputable. Remembering this, I took the name Nolan for my hero. I made my man the real man's brother. "He had spent half his youth with an older brother, hunting horses in Texas." And again: "He was catching wild horses in Texas with his adventurous cousin." I had the impression that Wilkinson's partner was named Stephen, and as Philip and Stephen were both evangelists in the Bible, as indeed I once heard a distinguished Episcopal divine preach a sermon about Philip on St. Stephen's day by accident, I named my man Philip Nolan, on the supposition that the mother who named one son Stephen would name another Philip. It was not for a year after, that, in looking at Wilkinson's *Memoirs* again, I found to my amazement, not to say my dismay, that Wilkinson's partner was named Philip Nolan. We had, therefore, two Philip Nolans, one a living historical character, who was shot by the Spaniards on the 21st of March, 1801 at Waco, Texas; the other a purely imaginary character, invented by myself, who appears for the first time on the 23rd of September, 1807, at a court-martial at Fort Adams.

Nobody but myself in New England had ever heard of Philip Nolan. But in the Southwest, in Texas and Louisiana, it was but sixty-two years since the Spaniards murdered him. In truth, it was the death of Nolan, the real Philip Nolan, killed by one Spanish governor while he held the safe-conduct of another, which roused that wave of indignation in the Southwest which ended in the independence of Texas. I think the State of Texas would do well, today, if it placed the statue of the real Phil Nolan in the Capitol at Washington by the side of that of Sam Houston.

Although we were at war, the *Atlantic* at once found its way into regions where the real Phil Nolan was known. A writer in the *New Orleans Picayune*, in a careful historical paper, explained at length that I had been mistaken all the way through, that Philip Nolan never went to sea, but to Texas. I received a letter from a lady in Baltimore who told me that two widowed sisters of his lived in that neighborhood. Unfortunately for me, this letter, written in perfectly good faith, was signed E. F. M. Fachtz. I was receiving many letters on the subject daily. I supposed that my correspondent was concealing her name, and was really "Eager for More Facts." When in reality I had the pleasure of meeting her a year or two afterwards, the two widowed sisters of the real Phil Nolan were both dead.

But in 1876 I was fortunate enough, on the kind invitation of Mr. Miner, to visit his family in their beautiful plantation at Terre Bonne. There I saw an old negro who was a boy when Master Phil Nolan left the old plantation on the Mississippi River for the last time. Master Phil Nolan had then married Miss Fanny Lintot, who was, I think, the aunt of my host. He permitted me to copy the miniature of the young adventurer.

I have since done my best to repair the error by which I gave Philip Nolan's name to another person, by telling the story of his fate in a book called *Philip Nolan's Friends*. For the purpose of that book, I studied the history of Miranda's attempt against Spain, and of John Adams's preparations for a descent of the Mississippi River. The professional historians of the United States are very reticent in their treatment of these themes. At the time when John Adams had a little army at Cincinnati, ready to go down and take New Orleans, there were no Western correspondents to the Eastern Press.

Within a year after the publication of the "Man Without a Country" in the *Atlantic*, more than half a million copies of the story had been printed in America and in England. I had curious accounts from the army and navy, of the interest with which it was read by gentlemen on duty. One of our officers lent the *Atlantic* to a lady in the Miner family. She ran into the parlor, crying out, "Here is a man who knows all about uncle Phil Nolan." An Ohio officer, who entered the city of Jackson, in Mississippi, with Grant, told me that he went at once to the State House. Matters were in a good deal of confusion there, and he picked up from the floor a paper containing the examination of Philip Nolan, at Walnut Springs, the old name of Vicksburg. This was before the real Philip's last expedition. The United States authorities, in the execution of the neutrality laws, had called him to account, and had made him show the evidence that he had the permission of the governor of New Orleans for his expedition.

In 1876 I visited Louisiana and Texas, to obtain material for *Philip Nolan's Friends*, which was published that year as a serial in *Scribner's Magazine*. I obtained there several autographs of the real Phil Nolan — and the original Spanish record of one of the trials of the survivors of his party — a trial which resulted in the cruel execution of Ephraim Blackburn, seven years after he was arrested. That whole transaction, wholly ignored by all historians of the United States known to me, is a sad blot on the American administration of the Spanish kings. Their excuse is the confusion of everything in Madrid between 1801 and 1807. The hatred of the Mexican authorities among our frontiersmen of the Southwest is largely due to the dishonor and cruelty of those transactions.

The Navy Department was occasionally asked what records it had of Phil Nolan's exile. Naturally, the gentlemen there did not like to confess ignorance. I was told, perhaps truly, that the answer generally given there was that "there was an officer kept on foreign service all his life, but that his name was not Nolan." A fine old friend of mine, an officer of marines, said seriously, when he read the story, that it was queer that while he had served on half the vessels in the service, he had never met this man. Another dear old friend of mine, president of a historical society, remembered the court-martial at Fort Adams very well. I am afraid no one else had any record of it.

Admiral Davis was good enough to tell me that the term "felucca" is not used outside the Straits of Gibraltar — and in the recent editions, as in this, the "felucca" with slaves is a "schooner." With one or two other such corrections the story in the reader's hands is the same as that published in the *Atlantic*, in 1863.

About twenty years ago, it was translated into German, with the omission of one or two passages, and published in a German journal. As soon as this magazine arrived here the story was retranslated, and reprinted as a German addition to American history, by the editor of the *American Magazine*. This was after half-a-million copies had been printed in the English language. The accident is an excellent illustration of the truth, that thus far no book has ever been published. It is to be wished that "publishers" could be made to understand this.

I learned, to my great pleasure, that it was translated into Spanish, and printed in Peru for the encouragement of the patriots of that country in their contest with Chile.

I have been glad to learn that it has proved a useful reading book in the higher classes of the schools in Minnesota, in Wisconsin, and other states.

— EDWARD E. HALE

Matunuck R.I.,
May 22, 1896

The Man Without A Country

I SUPPOSE that very few casual readers of the *New York Herald* of August 13, 1863, observed, in an obscure corner, among the "Deaths," the announcement:

> NOLAN. Died, on board U. S. Corvette *Levant*, Lat. 2° 11' S., Long. 131° W., on the 11th of May, PHILIP NOLAN.

I happened to observe it, because I was stranded at the old Mission House in Mackinaw, waiting for a Lake Superior steamer which did not choose to come, and I was devouring to the very stubble all the current literature I could get hold of, even down to the deaths and marriages in the *Herald*. My memory for names and people is good, and the reader will see, as he goes on, that I had reason enough to remember Philip Nolan. There are hundreds of readers who would have paused at that announcement, if the officer of the *Levant* who reported it had chosen to make it thus: "Died, May 11, THE MAN WITHOUT A COUNTRY."

For it was as "The Man Without a Country" that poor Philip Nolan had generally been known by the officers who had him in charge during some fifty years, as, indeed, by all the men who sailed under them. I dare say there is many a man who has taken wine with him once a fortnight, in a three-years' cruise, who never knew that his name was "Nolan," or whether the poor wretch had any name at all.

There can now be no possible harm in telling this poor creature's story. Reason enough there has been till now, ever since Madison's administration went out in 1817, for very strict secrecy, the secrecy of honor itself, among the gentlemen of the navy who have had Nolan in successive charge. And certainly it speaks well for the *esprit de corps* of the profession, and the personal honor of its members, that to the press this man's story has been wholly unknown — and, I think, to the country at large also. I have reason to think, from some investigations I made in the Naval Archives when I was attached to the Bureau of Construction, that every official report relating to him was burned when Ross burned the public buildings at Washington. One of the Tuckers, or possibly one of the Watsons, had Nolan in charge at the end of the war; and when, on returning from his cruise, he reported at Washington to one of the Crownin-shields — who was in the Navy Department when he came home — he found that the Department ignored the whole business. Whether they really knew nothing about it, or whether it was a *non mi ricordo*, determined on as a piece of policy, I do not know. But this I do know, that since 1817, and possibly before, no naval officer has mentioned Nolan in his report of a cruise.

But, as I say, there is no need for secrecy any longer. And now that the poor creature is dead, it seems to me worthwhile to tell a little of his story, by way of showing young Americans of today what it is to be A MAN WITHOUT A COUNTRY.

PHILIP NOLAN was as fine a young officer as there was in the "Legion of the West," as the western division of our army was then called. When Aaron Burr made his first dashing expedition down to New Orleans in 1805, at Fort Massac, or somewhere above on the river, he met, as the Devil would have it, this gay, dashing, bright young fellow at some dinner party, I think. Burr marked him, talked to him, walked with him, took him on a day or two's voyage in his flatboat, and, in short fascinated him. For the next year, barrack life was very tame to poor Nolan. He occasionally availed himself of the permission the great man had given him to write to him. Long, high-worded, stilted letters the poor boy wrote and rewrote and copied. But never a line did he have in reply from the gay deceiver. The other boys in the garrison sneered at him, because he sacrificed in this unrequited affection for a politician the time which they devoted to Monongahela, hazard, and high-low-jack. Bourbon, euchre, and poker were still unknown. But one day Nolan had his revenge. This time Burr came down the river, not as an attorney seeking a place for his office, but as a disguised conqueror. He had defeated I know not how many district attorneys; he had dined at I know not how many public dinners; he had been heralded in I know not how many Weekly Arguses, and it was rumored that he had an army behind him and an empire before him. It was a great day — his arrival — to poor Nolan. Burr had not been at the fort an hour before he sent for him. That evening he asked Nolan to take him out in his skiff, to show him a canebrake or a cottonwood tree, as he said — really to seduce him; and by the time the sail was over, Nolan was enlisted body and soul. From that time, though he did not yet know it, he lived as A MAN WITHOUT A COUNTRY.

What Burr meant to do I know no more than you, dear reader. It is none of our business just now. Only, when the grand catastrophe came, and Jefferson and the House of Virginia of that day undertook to break on the wheel all the possible Clarences of the then House of York, by the great treason trial at Richmond, some of the lesser fry in that distant Mississippi Valley, which was farther from us than Puget Sound is today, introduced the like novelty on their provincial stage; and, to while away the monotony of the summer at Fort Adams, got up, for *spectacles*, a string of court-martials on the officers there. One and another of the colonels and majors were tried, and, to fill out the list, little Nolan, against whom, Heaven knows, there was evidence enough — that he was sick of the service, had been willing to be false to it, and would have obeyed any order to march anywhere with anyone who would follow him had the order been signed, "By command of His Exc. A. Burr." The courts dragged on. The big flies escaped — rightly for all I know. Nolan was proved guilty enough, as I say; yet you and I would never have heard of him, reader, but that, when the president of the court asked him at the close whether he wished to say anything to show that he had always been faithful to the United States, he cried out, in a fit of frenzy, "Damn the United States! I wish I may never hear of the United States again!"

I suppose he did not know how the words shocked old Colonel Morgan, who was holding the court. Half the officers who sat in it had served through the Revolution, and their lives, not to say their necks, had been risked for the very idea which he so cavalierly cursed in his madness. He, on his part, had grown up in the West of those days, in the midst of "Spanish plot," "Orleans plot," and all the rest. He had been educated on a plantation where the finest company was a Spanish officer or a French merchant from Orleans. His education, such as it was, had been perfected in commercial expeditions to Vera Cruz, and I think he told me his father once hired an Englishman to be a private tutor for a winter on the plantation. He had spent half his youth with an older brother, hunting horses in Texas; and, in a word, to him "United States" was scarcely a reality. Yet he had been fed by "United States "for all the years since he had been in the army. He had sworn on his faith as a Christian to be true to "United States." It was "United States" which gave him the uniform he wore, and the sword by his side. Nay, my poor Nolan, it was only because "United States" had picked you out first as one of her own confidential men of honor that "A. Burr" cared for you a straw more than for the flat-boat men who sailed his ark for him. I do not excuse Nolan; I only explain to the reader why he damned his country, and wished he might never hear her name again.

He never did hear her name but once again. From that moment, September 23, 1807, till the day he died, May 11, 1863, he never heard her name again. For that half-century and more he was a man without a country.

Old Morgan, as I said, was terribly shocked. If Nolan had compared George Washington to Benedict Arnold, or had cried, "God save King George," Morgan would not have felt worse. He called the court into his private room, and returned in fifteen minutes, with a face like a sheet, to say, "Prisoner, hear the sentence of the Court! The Court decides, subject to the approval of the President, that you never hear the name of the United States again."

Nolan laughed. But nobody else laughed. Old Morgan was too solemn, and the whole room was hushed dead as night for a minute. Even Nolan lost his swagger in a moment. Then Morgan added, "Mr.

Marshal, take the prisoner to Orleans in an armed boat, and deliver him to the naval commander there."

The marshal gave his orders and the prisoner was taken out of court. "Mr. Marshal," continued old Morgan, "see that no one mentions the United States to the prisoner. Mr. Marshal, make my respects to Lieutenant Mitchell at Orleans and request him to order that no one shall mention the United States to the prisoner while he is on board ship. You will receive your written orders from the officer on duty here this evening. The court is adjourned without day."

I have always supposed that Colonel Morgan himself took the proceedings of the court to Washington city, and explained them to Mr. Jefferson. Certain it is that the President approved them — certain, that is, if I may believe the men who say they have seen his signature. Before the *Nautilus* got round from New Orleans to the northern Atlantic coast with the prisoner on board, the sentence had been approved, and he was a man without a country.

The plan then adopted was substantially the same which was necessarily followed ever after. Perhaps it was suggested by the necessity of sending him by water from Fort Adams and Orleans. The Secretary of the Navy — it must have been the first Crowninshield, though he is a man I do not remember — was requested to put Nolan on board a government vessel bound on a long cruise, and to direct that he should be only so far confined there as to make it certain that he never saw or heard of the country. We had few long cruises then, and the navy was very much out of favor; and as almost all of this story is traditional, as I have explained, I do not know certainly what his first cruise was. But the commander to whom he was entrusted — perhaps it was Tingey or Shaw, though I think it was one of the younger men — we are all old enough now — regulated the etiquette and the precautions of the affair, and according to his scheme they were carried out, I suppose, till Nolan died.

When I was second officer of the *Intrepid*, some thirty years after, I saw the original paper of instructions. I have been sorry ever since that I did not copy the whole of it. It ran, however, much in this way:

> WASHINGTON [with a date, which must have been late in 1807].
>
> SIR: You will receive from Lieutenant Neale the person of Philip Nolan, late a lieutenant in the United States Army.
>
> This person on his trial by court-martial expressed, with an oath, the wish that he might "never hear of the United States again."

The Court sentenced him to have his wish fulfilled.

For the present, the execution of the order is entrusted by the President to this Department.

You will take the prisoner on board your ship, and keep him there with such precautions as shall prevent his escape.

You will provide him with such quarters, rations, and clothing as would be proper for an officer of his late rank, if he were a passenger on your vessel on the business of his government.

The gentlemen on board will make any arrangements agreeable to themselves regarding his society. He is to be exposed to no indignity of any kind, nor is he ever unnecessarily to be reminded that he is a prisoner.

But under no circumstances is he ever to hear of his country or to see any information regarding it; and you will especially caution all the officers under your command to take care, that, in the various indulgences which may be granted, this rule, in which his punishment is involved, shall not be broken.

It is the intention of the government that he shall never again see the country which he has disowned. Before the end of your cruise you will receive orders which will give effect to this intention.

Respectfully yours,

W. SOUTHARD, for the
Secretary of the Navy

If I had only preserved the whole of this paper, there would be no break in the beginning of my sketch of this story. For Captain Shaw, if it were he, handed it to his successor in the charge, and he to his, and I suppose the commander of the *Levant* has it today as his authority for keeping this man in this mild custody.

The rule adopted on board the ships on which I have met "the man without a country" was, I think, transmitted from the beginning. No mess liked to have him permanently, because his presence cut off all talk of home or of the prospect of return, of politics or letters, of peace or of war — cut off more than half the talk men liked to have at sea. But it was always thought too hard that he should never meet the rest of us, except to touch hats, and we finally sank into one system. He was not permitted to talk with the men, unless an officer was by. With officers he had unrestrained intercourse, as far as they and he chose. But he grew shy, though he had favorites: I was one. Then the captain always asked him to dinner on Monday. Every mess in succession took up the invitation in its turn. According to the size of the ship, you had him at your mess more or less often at dinner. His breakfast he ate in his own stateroom — he always had a stateroom—which was where a sentinel or somebody on the watch could see the door. And whatever else he ate or drank, he ate or drank alone. Sometimes, when the marines or sailors had any special jollification, they were permitted to invite "Plain Buttons," as they called him. Then Nolan was sent with some officer, and the men were forbidden to speak of home while he was there. I believe the theory was that the sight of his punishment did them good. They called him "Plain-Buttons," because, while he always chose to wear a regulation army uniform, he was not permitted to wear the army button, for the reason that it bore either the initials or the insignia of the country he had disowned.

I remember, soon after I joined the navy, I was on shore with some of the older officers from our ship and from the *Brandywine*, which we had met at Alexandria. We had leave to make a party and go up to Cairo and the Pyramids. As we jogged along (you went on donkeys then), some of the gentlemen (we boys called them "Dons," but the phrase has long since changed) fell to talking about Nolan, and someone told the system which was adopted from the first about his books and other reading. As he was almost never permitted to go on shore even though the vessel lay in port for months, his time at the best hung heavy; and everybody was permitted to lend him books, if they were not published in America and made no allusion to it. These were common enough in the old days, when people in the other hemisphere talked of the United States as little as we do of Paraguay. He had almost all the foreign papers that came into the ship, sooner or later; only somebody must go over them first, and cut out any advertisement or stray paragraph that alluded to America. This was a little cruel sometimes, when the back of what was cut out might be as innocent as Hesiod. Right in the midst of one of Napoleon's battles, or one of Canning's speeches, poor Nolan would find a great hole, because on the back of the page of that paper there had been an advertisement of a packet for New York, or a scrap from the President's message. I say this was the first time I ever heard of this plan, which afterwards I had enough and more than enough to do with. I remember it, because poor Phillips, who was of the party, as soon as the allusion to reading was made, told a story of something which happened at the Cape of Good Hope on Nolan's first voyage; and it is the only thing I ever knew of that voyage. They had touched at the Cape, and had done the civil thing with the English admiral and the fleet, and then, leaving for a long cruise up the Indian Ocean, Phillips had borrowed a lot of English books from an officer, which, in those days, as indeed in these, was quite a windfall. Among them, as the Devil would order, was the *Lay of the Last Minstrel*, which they had all of them heard of, but which most of them had never seen. I think it could not have been published long. Well, nobody thought there could be any risk of anything national in that, though Phillips swore old Shaw had cut out the "Tempest" from Shakespeare before he let Nolan have it, because he said "the Bermudas ought to be ours, and, by Jove, should be one day." So Nolan was permitted to join the circle one afternoon when a lot of them sat on deck smoking and reading aloud. People do not do such things so often now; but when I was young we got rid of a great deal of time so. Well, so it happened that in his turn Nolan took the book and read to the others; and he read very well, as I know. Nobody in the circle knew a line of the poem, only it was all magic and Border chivalry, and was ten thousand years ago. Poor Nolan read steadily through the fifth canto, stopped a minute and drank something, and then began, without a thought of what was coming:

> Breathes there the man, with soul so dead,
> Who never to himself hath said:

It seems impossible to us that anybody ever heard this for the first time; but all these fellows did then, and poor Nolan himself went on, still unconsciously or mechanically:

> This is my own, my native land!"

Then they all saw something was to pay; but he expected to get through, I suppose, turned a little pale, but plunged on:

> Whose heart hath ne'er within him burned,
> As home his footsteps he hath turned
> From wandering on a foreign strand?
> If such there breathe, go, mark him well,

By this time the men were all beside themselves, wishing there was any way to make him turn over two pages; but he had not quite presence of mind for that; he gagged a little, colored crimson, and staggered on:

> "For him no minstrel raptures swell;
> High though his titles, proud his name,
> Boundless his wealth as wish can claim,
> Despite these titles, power, and pelf,
> The wretch, concentred all in self,

and here the poor fellow choked, could not go on, but started up, swung the book into the sea, vanished into his stateroom, "And by Jove," said Phillips, "we did not see him for two months again. And I had to make up some beggarly story to that English surgeon why I did not return his Walter Scott to him."

That story shows about the time when Nolan's braggadocio must have broken down. At first, they said, he took a very high tone, considered his imprisonment a mere farce, affected to enjoy the voyage, and all that; but Phillips said that after he came out of his state-room he never was the same man again. He never read aloud again, unless it was the Bible or Shakespeare, or something else he was sure of. But it was not that merely. He never entered in with the other young men exactly as a companion again. He was always shy afterwards, when I knew him — very seldom spoke, unless he was spoken to, except to a very few friends. He lighted up occasionally — I remember late in his life hearing him fairly eloquent on something which had been suggested to him by one of Fléchier's sermons — but generally he had the nervous, tired look of a heart-wounded man.

When Captain Shaw was coming home — if, as I say, it was Shaw — rather to the surprise of everybody they made one of the Windward Islands, and lay off and on for nearly a week. The boys said the officers were sick of saltjunk, and meant to have turtle-soup before they came home. But after several days the *Warren* came to the same rendezvous; they exchanged signals; she sent to Phillips and these homeward-bound men letters and papers, and told them she was outward-bound, perhaps to the Mediterranean, and took poor Nolan and his traps on the boat back to try his second cruise. He looked very blank when he was told to get ready to join her. He had known enough of the signs of the sky to know that till that moment he was going "home." But this was a distinct evidence of something he had not thought of, perhaps—that there was no going home for him, even to a prison. And this was the first of some twenty such transfers, which brought him sooner or later into half our best vessels, but which kept him all his life at least some hundred miles from the country he had hoped he might never hear of again.

It may have been on that second cruise—it was once when he was up the Mediterranean—that Mrs. Graff, the celebrated southern beauty of those days, danced with him. They had been lying a long time in the Bay of Naples, and the officers were very intimate in the English fleet, and there had been great festivities, and our men thought they must give a great ball on board the ship. How they ever did it on board the *Warren* I am sure I do not know. Perhaps it was not the *Warren*, or perhaps ladies did not take up so much room as they do now. They wanted to use Nolan's stateroom for something, and they hated to do it without asking him to the ball; so the captain said they might ask him, if they would be responsible that he did not talk with the wrong people, "who would give him intelligence." So the dance went on, the finest party that had ever been known, I dare say; for I never heard of a man-of-war ball that was not. For ladies they had the family of the American consul, one or two travellers who had adventured so far, and a nice bevy of English girls and matrons, perhaps Lady Hamilton herself.

Well, different officers relieved each other in standing and talking with Nolan in a friendly way, so as to be sure that nobody else spoke to him. The dancing went on with spirit, and after a while even the fellows who took this honorary guard of Nolan ceased to fear any contretemps. Only when some English lady — Lady Hamilton, as I said, perhaps — called for a set of "American dances," an odd thing happened. Everybody then danced contra-dances. The black band, nothing loath, conferred as to what "American dances" were, and started off with "Virginia Reel," which they followed with "Money-Musk," which, in its turn in those days, should have been followed by "The Old Thirteen." But just as Dick, the leader, tapped for his fiddles to begin, and bent forward, about to say, in true negro state, "'The Old Thirteen,' gentlemen and ladies!" as he had said "'Virginny Reel,' if you please!" and "'Money-Musk,' if you please!" the captain's boy tapped him on the shoulder, whispered to him, and he did not announce the name of the dance; he merely bowed, began on the air, and they all fell to — the officers teaching the English girls the figure, but not telling them why it had no name.

But that is not the story I started to tell. As the dancing went on, Nolan and our fellows all got at ease, as I said — so much so, that it seemed quite natural for him to bow to that splendid Mrs. Graff, and say, "I hope you have not forgotten me, Miss Rutledge. Shall I have the honor of dancing?"

He did it so quickly, that Fellows, who was with him, could not hinder him. She laughed and said, "I am not Miss Rutledge any longer, Mr. Nolan; but I will dance all the same," just nodded to Fellows, as if to say he must leave Mr. Nolan to her, and led him off to the place where the dance was forming.

Nolan thought he had got his chance. He had known her at Philadelphia, and at other places had met her, and this was a Godsend. You could not talk in contra-dances, as you do in cotillions, or even in the pauses of waltzing; but there were chances for tongues and sounds, as well as for eyes and blushes. He began with her travels, and Europe, and Vesuvius, and the French; and then, when they had worked down, and had that long talking time at the bottom of the set, he said boldly — a little pale, she said, as she told me the story years after:

"And what do you hear from home, Mrs. Graff?" And that splendid creature looked through him. Jove! How she must have looked through him!

"Home!! Mr. Nolan!!! I thought you were the man who never wanted to hear of home again!" and she walked directly up the deck to her husband, and left poor Nolan alone, as he always was. He did not dance again. I cannot give any history of him in order; nobody can now; and, indeed, I am not trying to.

These are the traditions, which I sort out, as I believe them, from the myths which have been told about this man for forty years. The lies that have been told about him are legion. The fellows used to say he was the "Iron Mask"; and poor George Pons went to his grave in the belief that this was the author of *Junius*, who was being punished for his celebrated libel on Thomas Jefferson. Pons was not very strong in the historical line.

A happier story than either of these I have told is of the war. That came along soon after. I have heard this affair told in three or four ways — and, indeed, it may have happened more than once. But which ship it was on I cannot tell. However, in one, at least, of the great frigate duels with the English, in which the navy was really baptized, it happened that a round-shot from the enemy entered one of our ports square, and took right down the officer of the gun himself, and almost every man of the gun's crew. Now you may say what you choose about courage, but that is not a nice thing to see. But, as the men who were not killed picked themselves up, and as they and the surgeon's people were carrying off the bodies, there appeared Nolan, in his shirtsleeves, with the rammer in his hand, and, just as if he had been the officer, told them off with authority — who should go to the cockpit with the wounded men, who should stay with him — perfectly cheery, and with that way which makes men feel sure all is right and is going to be right. And he finished loading the gun with his own hands, aimed it, and bade the men fire. And there he stayed, captain of that gun, keeping those fellows in spirits, till the enemy struck—sitting on the carriage while the gun was cooling, though he was exposed all the time—showing them easier ways to handle heavy shot—making the raw hands laugh at their own blunders—and when the gun cooled again, getting it loaded and fired twice as often as any other gun on the ship. The captain walked forward by way of encouraging the men, and Nolan touched his hat and said, "I am showing them how we do this in the artillery, sir."

And this is the part of the story where all the legends agree; the commodore said, "I see you do, and I thank you, sir; and I shall never forget this day, sir, and you never shall, sir."

And after the whole thing was over, and he had the Englishman's sword, in the midst of the state and ceremony of the quarterdeck, he said: "Where is Mr. Nolan? Ask Mr. Nolan to come here." And when Nolan came, he said, "Mr. Nolan, we are all very grateful to you today; you are one of us today; you will be named in the despatches."

And then the old man took off his own sword of ceremony, and gave it to Nolan, and made him put it on. The man told me this who saw it. Nolan cried like a baby, and well he might. He had not worn a sword since that infernal day at Fort Adams. But always afterwards on occasions of ceremony, he wore that quaint old French sword of the commodore's.

The captain did mention him in the despatches. It was always said he asked that he might be pardoned. He wrote a special letter to the Secretary of War. But nothing ever came of it. As I said, that was about the time when they began to ignore the whole transaction at Washington, and when Nolan's imprisonment began to carry itself on because there was nobody to stop it without any new orders from home.

I have heard it said that he was with Porter when he took possession of the Nukahiwa Islands. Not this Porter, you know, but old Porter, his father, Essex Porter — that is, the old Essex Porter, not this Essex. As an artillery officer, who had seen service in the West, Nolan knew more about fortifications, embrasures, ravelins, stockades, and all that, than any of them did; and he worked with a right goodwill in fixing that battery all right. I have always thought it was a pity Porter did not leave him in command there with Gamble. That would have settled all the question about his punishment. We should have kept the islands, and at this moment we should have one station in the Pacific Ocean. Our French friends, too, when they wanted this little watering place, would have found it was preoccupied. But Madison and the Virginians, of course, flung all that away.

All that was near fifty years ago. If Nolan was thirty then, he must have been near eighty when he died. He looked sixty when he was forty. But he never seemed to me to change a hair afterwards. As I imagine his life, from what I have seen and heard of it, he must have been in every sea, and yet almost never on land. He must have known, in a formal way, more officers in our service than any man living knows. He told me once, with a grave smile, that no man in the world lived so methodical a life as he. "You know the boys say I am the Iron Mask, and you know how busy he was." He said it did not do for anyone to try to read all the time, more than to do anything else all the time; but that he read just five hours a day. "Then," he said, "I keep up my notebooks, writing in them at such and such hours from what I have been reading; and I include in these my scrapbooks." These were very curious indeed. He had six or eight, of different subjects. There was one of History, one of Natural Science, one which he called "Odds and Ends." But they were not merely books of extracts from newspapers. They had bits of plants and ribbons, shells tied on, and carved scraps of bone and wood, which he had taught the men to cut for him, and they were beautifully illustrated. He drew admirably. He had some of the funniest drawings there, and some of the most pathetic, that I have ever seen in my life. I wonder who will have Nolan's scrapbooks.

Well, he said his reading and his notes were his profession, and that they took five hours and two hours respectively of each day. "Then," said he, "every man should have a diversion as well as a profession. My natural history is my diversion." That took two hours a day more. The men used to bring him birds and fish, but on a long cruise he had to satisfy himself with centipedes and cockroaches and such small game. He was the only naturalist I ever met who knew anything about the habits of the housefly and the mosquito. All those people can tell you whether they are *Lepidoptera* or *Steptopotera*; but as for telling how you can get rid of them, or how they get away from you when you strike them — why Linnæus knew as little of that as John Foy the idiot did. These nine hours made Nolan's regular daily "occupation." The rest of the time he talked or walked. Till he grew very old, he went aloft a great deal. He always kept up his exercise; and I never heard that he was ill. If any other man was ill, he was the kindest nurse in the world; and he knew more than half the surgeons do. Then if anybody was sick or died, or if the captain wanted him to, on any other occasion, he was always ready to read prayers. I have said that he read beautifully.

My own acquaintance with Philip Nolan began six or eight years after the English war, on my first voyage after I was appointed a midshipman. It was in the first days after our Slave Trade treaty, while the Reigning House, which was still the House of Virginia, had still a sort of sentimentalism about the suppression of the horrors of the Middle Passage, and something was sometimes done that way. We were in the South Atlantic on that business. From the time I joined, I believe I thought Nolan was a sort of lay chaplain — a chaplain with a blue coat. I never asked about him. Everything in the ship was strange to me. I knew it was green to ask questions, and I suppose I thought there was a "Plain-Buttons" on every ship. We had him to dine in our mess once a week, and the caution was given that on that day nothing was to be said about home. But if they had told us not to say anything about the planet Mars or the Book of Deuteronomy, I should not have asked why; there were a

great many things which seemed to me to have as little reason. I first came to understand anything about
"the man without a country" one day when we over-
hauled a dirty little schooner which had slaves on
board. An officer was sent to take charge of her, and,
after a few minutes, he sent back his boat to ask that
someone might be sent him who could speak Portuguese. We were all looking over the rail when the
message came, and we all wished we could interpret,
when the captain asked who spoke Portuguese. But
none of the officers did; and just as the captain was
sending forward to ask if any of the people could,
Nolan stepped out and said he should be glad to
interpret, if the captain wished, as he understood the
language. The captain thanked him, fitted out another boat with him, and in this boat it was my luck to go.

When we got there, it was such a scene as you
seldom see, and never want to. Nastiness beyond
account, and chaos run loose in the midst of the nastiness. There were not a great many of the negroes;
but by way of making what there were understand
that they were free, Vaughan had had their handcuffs
and ankle-cuffs knocked off, and, for convenience's
sake, was putting them upon the rascals of the
schooner's crew. The negroes were, most of them, out

of the hold, and swarming all round the dirty deck, with a central throng surrounding Vaughan and addressing him in every dialect, and *patois* of a dialect, from the Zulu click up to the Parisian of Beledel-jereed.

As we came on deck, Vaughan looked down from a hogshead, on which he had mounted in desperation, and said: "For God's love, is there anybody who can make these wretches understand something? The men gave them rum, and that did not quiet them. I knocked that big fellow down twice, and that did not soothe him. And then I talked Choctaw to all of them together; and I'll be hanged if they understood that as well as they understood the English."

Nolan said he could speak Portuguese, and one or two fine-looking Kroomen were dragged out, who, as it had been found already, had worked for the Portuguese on the coast at Fernando Po.

"Tell them they are free," said Vaughan; "and tell them that these rascals are to be hanged as soon as we can get rope enough."

Nolan "put that into Spanish," that is, he explained it in such Portuguese as the Kroomen could understand, and they in turn to such of the negroes as could understand them. Then there was such a yell of

delight, clinching of fists, leaping and dancing, kissing of Nolan's feet, and a general rush made to the
hogshead by way of spontaneous worship of Vaughan,
as the *deus ex machina* of the occasion.

"Tell them," said Vaughan, well pleased, "that I will
take them all to Cape Palmas."

This did not answer so well. Cape Palmas was
practically as far from the homes of most of them as
New Orleans or Rio de Janeiro was; that is, they
would be eternally separated from home there.

And their interpreters, as we could understand,
instantly said: "*Ah, non Palmas*," and began to propose
infinite other expedients in most voluble language.
Vaughan was rather disappointed at this result of his
liberality, and asked Nolan eagerly what they said.
The drops stood on poor Nolan's white forehead, as
he hushed the men down, and said, "He says, 'Not
Palmas.' He says, 'Take us home, take us to our own
country, take us to our own house, take us to our own
pickaninnies and our own women.' He says he has an
old father and mother who will die if they do not see
him. And this one says he left his people all sick, and
paddled down to Fernando to beg the white doctor to
come and help them, and that these devils caught him
in the bay just in sight of home, and that he has never

seen anybody from home since then. And this one says," choked out Nolan, "that he has not heard a word from his home in six months, while he has been locked up in an infernal barracoon."

Vaughan always said he grew gray himself while Nolan struggled through this interpretation. I, who did not understand anything of the passion involved in it, saw that the very elements were melting with fervent heat, and that something was to pay somewhere. Even the negroes themselves stopped howling, as they saw Nolan's agony, and Vaughan's almost equal agony of sympathy. As quick as he could get words, he said, "Tell them yes, yes, yes; tell them they shall go to the Mountains of the Moon, if they will. If I sail the schooner through the Great White Desert, they shall go home!"

And after some fashion Nolan said so. And then they all fell to kissing him again, and wanted to rub his nose with theirs.

But he could not stand it long; and getting Vaughan to say he might go back, he beckoned me down into our boat. As we lay back in the sternsheets and the men gave way, he said to me, "Youngster, let that show you what it is to be without a family, without a home, and without a country. And if you are ever tempted to say a word or to do a thing that shall put a bar between you and your family, your home, and your country, pray God in his mercy to take you that instant home to his own heaven. Stick by your family, boy; forget you have a self, while you do everything for them. Think of your home, boy; write and send, and talk about it. Let it be nearer and nearer to your thought, the farther you have to travel from it; and rush back to it when you are free, as that poor black slave is doing now. And for your country, boy," and the words rattled in his throat, "and for that flag," and he pointed to the ship, "never dream a dream but of serving her as she bids you, though the service carry you through a thousand hells. No matter what happens to you, no matter who flatters you or who abuses you, never look at another flag, never let a night pass but you pray God to bless that flag. Remember, boy, that behind all these men you have to do with, behind officers, and government, and people even, there is the Country Herself, your Country, and that you belong to Her as you belong to your own mother. Stand by Her, boy, as you would stand by your mother, if those devils there had got hold of her today!"

I was frightened to death by his calm, hard passion; but I blundered out that I would, by all that was holy, and that I had never thought of doing anything else. He hardly seemed to hear me; but he did, almost in a whisper, say, "Oh, if anybody had said so to me when I was of your age."

I think it was this half-confidence of his, which I never abused, for I never told this story till now, which afterward made us great friends. He was very kind to me. Often he sat up, or even got up, at night, to walk the deck with me, when it was my watch. He explained to me a great deal of my mathematics, and I owe to him my taste for mathematics. He lent me books and helped me about my reading. He never alluded so directly to his story again; but from one and another officer I have learned, in thirty years, what I am telling. When we parted from him in St. Thomas harbor, at the end of our cruise, I was more sorry than I can tell. I was very glad to meet him again in 1830; and later in life, when I thought I had some influence in Washington, I moved heaven and earth to have him discharged. But it was like getting a ghost out of prison. They pretended there was no such man, and never was such a man. They will say so at the Department now! Perhaps they do not know. It will not be the first thing in the service of which the Department appears to know nothing!

There is a story that Nolan met Burr once on one of our vessels, when a party of Americans came on board in the Mediterranean. But this I believe to be a lie; or, rather, it is a myth, *ben trovato*, involving a tremendous blowing-up with which he sunk Burr — asking him how he liked to be "without a country." But it is clear from Burr's life, that nothing of the sort could have happened; and I mention this only as an illustration of the stories which get a'going where there is the least mystery at bottom.

So poor Philip Nolan had his wish fulfilled. I know but one fate more dreadful; it is the fate reserved for those men who shall have one day to exile themselves from their country because they have attempted her ruin, and shall have at the same time to see the prosperity and honor to which she rises when she has rid herself of them and their iniquities. The wish of poor Nolan, as we all learned to call him, not because his punishment was too great, but because his repentance was so clear, was precisely the wish of every Bragg and Beauregard who broke a soldier's oath two years ago, and of every Maury and Barron who broke a sailor's. I do not know how often they have repented. I do know that they have done all that in them lay that they might have no country — that all the honors, associations, memories, and hopes which belong to "country" might be broken up into little shreds and distributed to the winds. I know, too, that their punishment, as they vegetate through what is left of life to them in wretched Boulognes and Leicester Squares, where they are destined to upbraid each other till they die, will have all the agony of Nolan's, with the added pang that every one who sees them will see them to despise and to execrate them. They will have their wish, like him.

For him, poor fellow, he repented of his folly, and then, like a man, submitted to the fate he had asked for. He never intentionally added to the difficulty or delicacy of the charge of those who had him in hold. Accidents would happen; but they never happened from his fault. Lieutenant Truxton told me that, when Texas was annexed, there was a careful discussion among the officers, whether they should get hold of Nolan's handsome set of maps and cut Texas out of it — from the map of the world and the map of Mexico. The United States had been cut out when the atlas was bought for him. But it was voted, rightly enough, that to do this would be virtually to reveal to him what had happened, or, as Harry Cole said, to make him think Old Burr had succeeded. So it was from no fault of Nolan's that a great botch happened at my own table, when, for a short time, I was in command of the *George Washington* corvette, on the South American station. We were lying in the La Plata, and some of the officers, who had been on shore and had just joined again, were entertaining us with accounts of their misadventures in riding the half-wild horses of Buenos Ayres. Nolan was at table, and was in an unusually bright and talkative mood. Some story of a tumble reminded him of an adventure of his own when he was catching wild horses in Texas with his adventurous cousin, at a time when he must have been quite a boy. He told the story with a good deal of spirit — so much so, that the silence which often follows a good story hung over the table for an instant, to be broken by Nolan himself. For he asked perfectly unconsciously, "Pray, what has become of Texas? After the Mexicans got their independence, I thought that province of Texas would come forward very fast. It is really one of the finest regions on earth; it is the Italy of this continent. But I have not seen or heard a word of Texas for near twenty years."

There were two Texan officers at the table. The reason he had never heard of Texas was that Texas and her affairs had been painfully cut out of his newspapers since Austin began his settlements; so that, while he read of Honduras and Tamaulipas, and, till quite lately, of California — this virgin province, in which his brother had travelled so far, and, I believe, had died, had ceased to be to him. Waters and Williams, the two Texas men, looked grimly at each other and tried not to laugh. Edward Morris had his attention attracted by the third link in the chain of the captain's chandelier. Watrous was seized with a convulsion of sneezing. Nolan himself saw that something was to pay, he did not know what. And I, as master of the feast had to say, "Texas is out of the map, Mr. Nolan. Have you seen Captain Back's curious account of Sir Thomas Roe's Welcome?"

After that cruise I never saw Nolan again. I wrote to him at least twice a year, for in that voyage we became even confidentially intimate; but he never wrote to me. The other men tell me that in those fifteen years he *aged* very fast, as well he might indeed, but that he was still the same gentle, uncomplaining, silent sufferer that he ever was, bearing as best he could his self-appointed punishment — rather less social, perhaps, with new men whom he did not know, but more anxious, apparently, than ever to serve and befriend and teach the boys, some of whom fairly seemed to worship him. And now it seems the dear old fellow is dead. He has found a home at last, and a country.

Since writing this, and while considering whether or no I would print it, as a warning to the young Nolans and Vallandighams and Tatnalls of today of what it is to throw away a country, I have received from Danforth, who is on board the *Levant*, a letter which gives an account of Nolan's last hours. It removes all my doubts about telling this story.

To understand the first words of the letter, the non-professional reader should remember that after 1817, the position of every officer who had Nolan in charge was one of the greatest delicacy. The government had failed to renew the order of 1807 regarding him. What was a man to do? Should he let him go? What, then, if he were called to account by the Department for violating the order of 1807? Should he keep him? What, then, if Nolan should be liberated some day, and should bring an action for false imprisonment or kidnapping against every man who had had him in charge? I urged and pressed this upon Southard, and I have reason to think that other officers did the same thing. But the Secretary always said, as they so often do at Washington, that there were no special orders to give, and that we must act on our own judgment. That means, "If you succeed, you will be sustained; if you fail, you will be disavowed." Well, as Danforth says, all that is over now, though I do not know but I expose myself to a criminal prosecution on the evidence of the very revelation I am making. Here is the letter:

LEVANT, 2° 2'S. @ 131° W.

DEAR FRED:

I try to find heart and life to tell you that it is all over with dear old Nolan. I have been with him on this voyage more than I ever was, and I can understand wholly now the way in which you used to speak of the dear old fellow. I could see that he was not strong, but I had no idea the end was so near. The doctor has been watching him very carefully, and yesterday morning came to me and told me that Nolan was not so well, and had not left his stateroom — a thing I never remember before. He had let the doctor come and see him as he lay there — the first time the doctor had been in the stateroom — and he said he should like to see me. Oh, dear! do you remember the mysteries we boys used to invent about his room in the old *Intrepid* days? Well, I went in, and there, to be sure, the poor fellow lay in his berth, smiling pleasantly as he gave me his hand, but looking very frail. I could not help a glance round, which showed me what a little shrine he had made of the box he was lying in. The stars and stripes were triced up above and around a picture of Washington, and he had painted a majestic eagle with lightnings blazing from his beak and his foot just clasping the whole globe, which his wings overshadowed. The dear old boy saw my glance, and said, with a sad smile, "Here, you see, I have a country!" And then he pointed to the foot of his bed, where I had not seen before a great map of the United States, as he had drawn it from memory, and which he had there to look upon as he lay. Quaint, queer old names were on it, in large letters: "Indiana Territory," "Mississippi Territory," and "Louisiana Territory," as I suppose our fathers learned such things: but the old fellow had patched in Texas, too; he had carried his western boundary all the way to the Pacific, but on that shore he had defined nothing.

"Oh Danforth," he said, "I know I am dying. I cannot get home. Surely you will tell me something now? — Stop! Stop! Do not speak till I say what I am sure you know, that there is not in this ship, that there is not in America — God bless her! — a more loyal man than I. There cannot be a man who loves the old flag as I do, or prays for it as I do, or hopes for it as I do. There are thirty-four stars in it now, Danforth. I thank God for that, though I do not know what their names are. There has never been one taken away: I thank

God for that. I know by that that there has never been any successful Burr. Oh Danforth, Danforth," he sighed out, "how like a wretched night's dream a boy's idea of personal fame or of separate sovereignty seems, when one looks back on it after such a life as mine! But tell me — tell me something — tell me everything, Danforth, before I die!"

Ingham, I swear to you that I felt like a monster that I had not told him everything before. Danger or no danger, delicacy or no delicacy, who was I, that I should have been acting the tyrant all this time over this dear, sainted old man, who had years ago expiated, in his whole manhood's life, the madness of a boy's treason? "Mr Nolan," said I, "I will tell you everything you ask about. Only, where shall I begin?"

Oh, the blessed smile that crept over his white face! And he pressed my hand and said, "God bless you! Tell me their names," he said, and he pointed to the stars on the flag. "The last I know is Ohio. My father lived in Kentucky. But I have guessed Michigan and Indiana and Mississippi — that was where Fort Adams is — they make twenty. But where are your other fourteen? You have not cut up any of the old ones, I hope?"

Well, that was not a bad text, and I told him the names in as good order as I could, and he bade me take down his beautiful map and draw them in as I best could with my pencil. He was wild with delight about Texas, told me how his cousin died there; he had marked a gold cross near where he supposed his grave was; and he had guessed at Texas. Then he was delighted as he saw California and Oregon — that, he said, he had suspected partly, because he had never been permitted to land on that shore, though the ships were there so much. "And the men," said he, laughing, "brought off a good deal besides furs." Then he went back — heavens, how far! — to ask about the Chesapeake, and what was done to Barron for surrendering her to the Leopard, and whether Burr ever tried again — and he ground his teeth with the only passion he showed. But in a moment that was over, and he said, "God forgive me, for I am sure I forgive him." Then he asked about the old war — told me the true story of his serving the gun the day we took the Java — and asked about dear old David Porter, as he called him. Then he settled down more quietly, and very happily, to hear me tell in an hour the history of fifty years.

How I wished it had been somebody who knew something! But I did as well as I could. I told him of the English war. I told him about Fulton and the steamboat beginning. I told him about old Scott, and Jackson; told him all I could think of about the Mississippi, and New Orleans, and Texas, and his own old Kentucky. And do you think, he asked who was in command of the "Legion of the West." I told him it was a very gallant officer named Grant, and that, by our last news, he was about to establish his headquarters at Vicksburg. Then, "Where was Vicksburg?" I worked that out on the map; it was about a hundred miles, more or less, above his old Fort Adams; and I thought Fort Adams must be a ruin now. "It must be at old Vick's plantation, at Walnut Hills," said he, "well, that is a change!"

I tell you, Ingham, it was a hard thing to condense the history of half a century into that talk with a sick man. And I do not now know what I told him — of emigration, and the means of it — of steamboats, and railroads, and telegraphs — of inventions, and books, and literature — of the colleges, and West Point, and the Naval School — but with the queerest interruptions that ever you heard. You see it was Robinson Crusoe asking all the accumulated questions of fifty-six years!

I remember he asked, all of a sudden, who was President now; and when I told him, he asked if Old Abe was General Benjamin Lincoln's son. He said he met old General Lincoln, when he was quite a boy himself, at some Indian treaty. I said no, that Old Abe was a Kentuckian like himself, but I could not tell him of what family; he had worked up from the ranks. "Good for him!" cried Nolan, "I am glad of that. As I have brooded and wondered, I have thought our danger was in keeping up those regular successions in the first families." Then I got talking about my visit to Washington. I told him of meeting the Oregon Congressman, Harding; I told him about the Smithsonian, and the Exploring Expedition; I told him about the Capitol, and the statues for the pediment, and Crawford's Liberty, and Greenough's Washington. Ingham, I told him everything I could think of that would show the grandeur of his country and its prosperity; but I could not make up my mouth to tell him a word about this infernal rebellion!

And he drank it in and enjoyed it as I cannot tell you. He grew more and more silent, yet I never thought he was red or faint. I gave him a glass of water, but he just wet his lips, and told me not to go away. Then he asked me to bring the Presbyterian *Book of Public Prayer*, which lay there, and said, with a smile, that it would open at the right place — and so it did. There was his double red mark down the page; and I knelt down and read, and he repeated with me, "For ourselves and our country, O gracious God, we thank Thee, that, notwithstanding our manifold transgressions of Thy holy laws, Thou hast continued to us Thy marvellous kindness . . .," and so to the end of that thanksgiving. Then he turned to the end of the same book, and I read the words more familiar to me: "Most heartily we beseech Thee with Thy favor to behold and bless Thy servant, the President of the United States, and all others in authority and the rest of the Episcopal collect."

"Danforth," said he, "I have repeated those prayers night and morning, it is now fifty-five years." And then he said he would go to sleep. He bent me down over him and kissed me; and he said, "Look in my Bible, Danforth, when I am gone." And I went away.

But I had no thought it was the end. I thought he was tired and would sleep. I knew he was happy, and I wanted him to be alone.

But in an hour, when the doctor went in gently, he found Nolan had breathed his life away with a smile. He had something pressed close to his lips. It was his father's badge of the Order of the Cincinnati.

We looked in his Bible, and there was a slip of paper at the place where he had marked the text: "They desire a country, even a heavenly: wherefore God is not ashamed to be called their God: for He hath prepared for them a city."

On this slip of paper he had written: "Bury me in the sea; it has been my home, and I love it. But will not someone set up a stone for my memory at Fort Adams or at Orleans, that my disgrace may not be more than I ought to bear? Say on it:

In Memory of
PHILIP NOLAN
Lieutenant in the Army of the United States.
He loved his country as no other man has
loved her; but no man deserved less at
her hands.

COLOPHON

THIS EDITION was designed and typeset by Scott-Martin Kosofsky at The Philidor Company in Boston. The types are Adobe Caslon, designed by Carol Twombly for Adobe Systems, and, for display, Elephant designed by Matthew Carter. Each was based on 18th- and 19th-century English types that enjoyed great popularity in early America. The wood engravings are from the 1832 catalogue of the Boston Type and Stereotype Foundry.

The imagesetting was by Aurora Graphics, Portsmouth, New Hampshire. The book was printed and bound by Sheridan Books, Fredericksburg, Virginia.